Wrong Person Always

Wrong person always copyright © 2025 by Courtney Louise, all rights reserved. Printed in Australia, no part of this book may be used or reproduced without written permission, except in the case of reprints or in the context of reviews.

ISBN: 978-0-646-72256-6 Imprint: Courts Books

Wrong person always

Courtney Louise

Wrong person always, is a love letter to the version of you that believed their lies.

It is incredibly heartfelt, full of raw emotion, heartbreak, hope, and self-healing. It is deeply personal and reads like a powerful emotional journey.

This book captures the pain of loving the wrong person, the struggle to let go, and the strength it takes to move forward.

Wrong Person Always is a testament to resilience. It's for anyone who has loved deeply, lost painfully, and still found the courage to rise. This book is my heart on paper; may it remind you that you are never alone in your healing.

—Courtney Louise

Contents

The Falling...12

The Fractured...48

The Recovery...107

The Falling

*By far, you were my favourite wrong person
You were so different, so inviting
Not my usual type, but I claimed you anyway*

*The perfect ten, while I was a six
For a while, you were mine*

When I first saw you,
I knew you weren't right for me

You were the type I knew would hurt me,
Yet I let you in anyway

Time passed, and I never thought I'd see you again
Until one day, there you were

Across the floor, looking at me
You approached me, and I went along,
We spoke words, and..

The crowded noise around me
Became silent and faint
Like, we were the only ones there

A follow. A follow-back
The first domino falling

Days became nights, then quickly,
You were all I thought about

Your voice, your smile,
The way you looked at me, it all felt like magic

But magic is just an illusion,
And illusions fade.

*I don't know what it was about you
That made me want more
You had something special that I loved*

*I knew we weren't good together
Yet I craved you like a child*

*Reaching for forbidden candy
Sticky hands, sour regret*

I am still lost in thought about you
Wondering how you are and what you are doing
Days go by so fast, you're still on my mind

My mind haunted by your ghost
Reminding me you exist

Imagining you in my bed
Imagining laughing with you
Imagining the late-night drives together

Imagining us together as a couple
Imagining meeting your family
Imagining taking vacations

Imagining you randomly calling me
Imagining the good morning/goodnight texts
Imagining buying you gifts just because I was thinking of you

Slowly with time, I felt myself falling for you
I wondered why and how feelings grew

Yet I opened my heart and let it happen
Soon, I trusted you and wanted you to stay

Every day, I ached to see you
And every night, your presence was my peace

You were my happiness and joy
You made my world light up like the stars

The ding of your "on your way" text
Made my heart feel warm

Your face at my door
Were my prayers being answered
Our messages daily were my devotions

Holding your hand for the first time
It was magical, and I felt complete
like a mother cradling her newborn

From that moment, I knew you were important
I'd never known a love like this before

Never tasted that sweetness,
Never got that magical feeling of loving someone

*Your problems are sealed within my mind
Like my favourite song lyrics, I'll never forget*

*Even though you thought I was somewhere else
I felt important to know your demons*

*I sat speechless, unable to provide the words
You wanted to hear, now I whisper
My responses to the mirror*

*The way you called me crazy
You confused, crazy for love*

*Called me too much
When it was me caring about you*

*All those conversations we could never have
Now I speak these conversations aloud
To the empty walls around me*

I want to cry because my mind is consumed by you
Tears fall down my face like rain dripping down a window

If a clock could be turned backwards
I'd rewrite our story with a better ending

This pain in my chest?
You mattered more to me then,
Silence can hold

I wonder if your thoughts
Whisper my name in your ear

Maybe I was too much for you
Maybe I wasn't good enough

Maybe I wasn't skinny enough
Maybe I wasn't pretty enough

Maybe I wasn't like other girls

*Can we go back to the time spent together
I crave those days so much more than you know*

*Those days made me feel the happiest I've been
The feeling I have now is alone and empty*

*The pain hurts so much,
but I know it's for the best*

I miss you. Do you miss me too?
You said you loved me
I believed you.

But love doesn't disappear overnight,
Doesn't leave you questioning your worth.

You walked away like I was nothing,
Like we were nothing

Just another game to a
heartless boy.

My heart aches to speak and hear from you
I look for you at the places we would go
Mapping them out in case you appear

To memorise your face and
Our final chance to say our goodbyes

Those were my happiest days
I never wanted them to end

But sadly..

They did
They ended like I never existed

*I will cherish the memories we shared
Maybe one day we will meet again*

*Till then,
 I will remember everything about you*

*Your face lives in my mind
like a bad headache I can't get rid of*

Your cute smile
Your beautiful eyes

Your laugh
The way your voice sounds

The way you would look at me
The way you make me feel
The way you make me blush

*Seeing you last night hurt
When I still have love for you*

*You brushed up against my arm
So I knew you were there
Walking past me like I didn't exist*

*My whole body froze when I saw your face
My heart broke while yours was whole*

*I wish we had never crossed paths
So this broken heart could not feel pain*

We came back together
Once again, my life was filled with joy

I missed you so much
This time was different, but my love hadn't changed
Although it was different, I still felt the pain

Our love felt so perfect
Every moment with you lit up my world again

As days went by, my heart fell deeper
Lost in your presence, feeling treasured

You were everything to me; no one else existed

*You promised to trust me
So I chose to trust you*

*We were meant to be
The thought of us together filled me with joy*

*Knowing you were going to be mine
Nothing else mattered
Just you*

The moment I knew you'd be mine
It was the sweetest joy I'd ever felt

Every dream was falling into place
Like the final piece of a puzzle
Completing the picture of us

Spending time with you once again was happiness
Even if our time was short, seeing you was enough
Those moments spent with you

More precious than anything
Filled with happiness no one else could fill

You were my happiness
You were my life

You were my best friend
You were my shooting star

You were my one true love

I loved you more than myself
That probably wasn't the best idea

You meant the whole world to me
No one could ever fill your place

*You were my sunshine
My light breaking through buildings*

*My love was brought back to life
When I feared I could never again*

*Our smiles and laughs
Our happiness brought together*

*Seeing you made my heart bloom
Filled me with a warm sensation*

*Only you could make it beat this way
Made it feel whole and complete*

Like finding my safe place in a disaster

What is my life without you?

Moving on would be impossible
Without you, I'm lost in the dark

Forgetting you would mean forgetting who I am
Time would go by, but I'd never unlove you

*One day, we could be soulmates
The perfect couple everyone talks about*

I'd call you husband, you'd call me your wife

*Life would be simple for us
Maybe one day that time would come*

I stare at the ceiling, wondering about the life we never had
We were happy together, it wasn't just imagination

I wonder if you'd fight for me like I did for you
Only to be left more damaged than before

But what I wonder the most..
Was any of it real?

*I wish we could just be together
But life is so cruel and unfair*

*You're the only one I want
You felt at home*

*A safe place to rest my peace
I wish you could see that I'm yours
Even though you are not mine*

*Maybe you didn't love me
Maybe I was just a game to you*

*Maybe you just used me
Maybe I was just filling a void*

Maybe I was a sidepiece

The Fractured

*Why did you give me false hope
When you knew you didn't want me*

*Why did you say I love you
Just to stab me in the back*

*Why did you let me cling to hope
When you wouldn't be mine to keep*

Was destroying my heart worth it?

If you wanted me, why did you make it hard?
I would've stayed

Loved you without conditions
Without chaos, without games

You made it seem like it was a chore to be with me
Like you didn't want to take part in

If I had a time machine to start over
I would change the way everything went

I'd either erase meeting you or
I'd erase the bad memories

For our story to start over

How do I unlove the person who's my world?

*How will mornings exist
Without your good morning message*

*How does my heart keep pumping
When my soul isn't there*

*This wound will be left open
While the nights drag on*

*I'll be left hollow
from where you used to be*

*Knowing that I will always love you is hard
Because time will keep on ticking and*

*You will always mean the world to me
And I will be happy for you*

*So find your happiness
I'll keep ours safe in my heart*

Did you even care?
When you shattered my heart

While tears poured out of me
Turning my life into a sad love song

No. You didn't

You just ripped out my heart
And never looked back

You had my love, but you chose to throw it away
I was loyal to you, but you wanted an unfaithful girl

An unfaithful girl wouldn't stay the way I did
But I still chased you

Clinging onto your rope that led me down a rabbit hole

You hid behind your troubles
Keeping it as an excuse to hurt me

But love doesn't hurt the heart that holds it

No storm in your life
Could justify the lightning you left me with

Every word spoken was a lie
You never loved me

You craved my comfort and affection
While I waited endlessly for your reply

Left me to drown in my thoughts
Reaching out to those who would never care deeply
Like I did..

Counting every second, minute, hour, waiting for you
Foolish of me to believe you cared

Your actions spoke louder
I've learnt my lesson now

You weren't worth the time I wasted

Would those girls stay with you like I did
Would they stay even at your worst, like I did

Would they care the way I did about you
Would they let you treat them how you treated me

Or would they leave whole, unlike me

*You acted like a boyfriend
But you didn't want to be one*

*Said you couldn't sleep next to anyone
Yet my sheets still smell of you*

Was I just another anyone?

All you did was lie
Lie, lie and lie

Did that make you feel powerful?

The fuel to your ego
I hope it was worth the burn

*Thank you for the lessons
Thank you for the pain*

*You created me into a woman
You no longer deserve*

*Sadly, you don't get to keep her
Thank you for the upgrade
The next man will cherish*

*They won't love you like I did
They'll kiss you, but not your scars*

*They'll hold you, but not your chaos
They'll care, but only when it's easy*

*And you? You'll always miss me
Because they'll never be me*

*If you called me
I'd still answer, after the damage*

*Telling myself I wouldn't
When we both know that's a lie*

*I still love you
Not who you are, but the version I created*

*Will I forget you?
No.*

But the day will come when I stop wishing you would remember me

I lie awake replaying the moments in my mind
Sleep is hard, I keep wondering if you ever think of me
I know you don't, but foolishly, I have hope

Maybe you miss me
Maybe tonight, I'll get that text with your name
But it never comes

You moved on like I meant nothing
Like we meant nothing.

How could you do this to someone?
You swore you loved?
Was it all a lie?

Every word is empty
Every touch is fake
Every promise broken

Why?
Just tell me why

Was I that easy to forget?

*Days keep going by
feeling foolish for wanting you*

*Another wrong person
Another dead end*

But this time, I learn:

*No more trust,
No more chances,
No more of myself left to break*

*"I'll love you forever, sadly
Even if I let go, the love remains
Too heavy for tears, too deep for pain
Now my heart bleeds in silence, numb."*

*I should've listened to my friends
They saw the red flags before I did*

*But I believed in your good
Blind to the cost of trust*

Now, we are just strangers with memories

Why did you act like you wanted me?
Why did you act like you cared?
Why did you always keep coming back?

When all you did was lie and play games

*Foolish of me to trust your lies
Claimed that you spoke to no one*

*I always knew the truth
You proved it again and again*

Yet I still came back

I'll never stop loving you
Deep down, a part of me can't let go

But after all the pain I endured
You're nothing now...

Just a stranger I used to know

Last night, I stayed awake till 6 am
Maybe I was afraid to fall asleep

Because if I dream, it might be about you
And I can't stomach seeing you there again

I just want to erase you from my mind

Your feelings were a joke
And mine were real

Now I'm left shattered
Fixing the damage you broke
Like broken glass shattered on the floor

*Rage burning inside me
I long to cry,*

*But the tears don't fall
Because crying for you
Would change nothing at all*

*I passed by your place today
There you were ...*

*But I couldn't glance your way
Unable to meet your eyes*

*Even though I wish too
I couldn't let myself try*

I prayed to god every day about you
I asked if you weren't for me

for him to remove you
But we always kept coming back

Why? Was my pain your energy
Or did my pain make you feel joy?

I waited, staring at my phone
Hoping for a reply from you

But you never did, why?
Because I don't exist to you
Just a ghost...

A want, but I'm left alone
Yet still, I ache for one word from you

*Three days of silence, feeling lost
Drowning in my mind, I can't resist*

*Still checking my phone, hoping
Your name will appear, but it's clear*

It's finally over for us, we're through

*I'm sorry for the unwanted pain I caused you
I was hurting too, and it flowed over*

*I never wanted to hurt you
Not when I loved you
Not when I still do*

*If I could erase the pain, I would
That wasn't me, and never meant to be me*

The day you told me you didn't want to speak anymore
My heart broke, and my tears fell

I was losing a part of me, I wasn't ready to
You were so important to me

I wasn't prepared to let you go
I thought we had more time left together

Maybe in another life, we were meant to be
Just not this one, and that's what hurts

*You said you were cutting off everyone, even me!
Was I just like everyone else to you?*

*Is that all I was?
Just another person who meant nothing?*

*I thought I was more than that
But now you said that just meant I wasn't*

I wish I could've been the person for you
Like you were that person for me

But you never even tried
Just tossed me to the side like I was nothing

Like I was an old piece of gum
Disgusting and worthless
Stuck beneath your shoe

*I have my regrets
Knowing I hurt you, cut me deep*

*But because I loved you, I fought
I gave everything
Only to realise…*

*No matter how hard I tried
I'd never be enough
Never the one you wanted to keep*

Days keep going by
I don't know why I bother
Trying to reach out

Hoping for something
When you don't care

The silence is so loud
You reply so dry, like I'm nothing
Guess that's all I am to you now

*I sit alone in my car
While you're running on my mind*

*I still care about you that much
But you?*

*You probably already moved on
Without giving me a second thought*

*I guess that's the difference between us
I loved you in a way you never loved me*

When I look at the stars, I imagine you
You were the stars in my sky
You lit up my world, filling it with warmth

That's why they remind me of you
That's why the stars are my favourite
And why the night feels like yours

*Tonight, I sat in the car and cried my heart out
My chest aching with pain*

*If only you could see how damaged you made me
You tore my heart out like it was so easy,
Like I was nothing*

*If I could just stop the tears, I would
But they won't let me*

*The love I gave you
Almost destroyed me*

*Piece by piece, I disappeared
Not knowing who I even was anymore*

*Alone and drowning
Wishing I could end it all*

*I poured everything into you
What a waste of my time*

*I thought you were worth it
But now I see clearly*

*You never deserved it
I was always too much for you*

Maybe it's not even you I miss
Maybe it's the version of you I created

Because in my head, you were different
And that version wouldn't hurt me
That version gave me the world

Oh, how it would be to stop caring and crying

Who am I anymore?
The days are so lonely

Not a day without crying
My heart keeps breaking

Today I let you go
No more hurting myself trying and hoping

because that day will never come
So, from now on, I will close the door behind me
This is me walking away

*The voice message I sent
Those words will be my last*

*No more words to say
because they mean nothing*

*Just words to you
I put myself first now*

*Memories we shared, I'll never forget
That's all they are now: memories*

God knows I'll be okay because he's got me

*Songs will bring back memories
But that's okay, no more shedding tears*

*I sit here wondering, should I reach out?
One last 'I wish you the best' before we die out*

But hitting 'send' means it's goodbye...

*Am I ready to let go?
Am I prepared to try?*

Today, the day I cut the rope
No more lies, no more pain

I'm done
I don't care anymore

To me, you're a stranger
Just a stranger I used to know

*Tonight, the clock strikes midnight
This year, you stay in the past*

*If only you could come with me
But enough time has already been wasted*

*My love won't fade, this is the truth
Even though I'll never be enough for you*

*Romance films hurt in a way I can't ignore
Every scene pulls you back to me*

*We had that once... soft radiances, perfect love
Now, just flashes of what I thought would stand*

*I watch love stories like flipping through scars,
We wrote those pages
Then left them to be unread*

I pulled into the parking lot we knew by heart
Sitting here alone, the memories flood back

This place holds joy and pain, both just as plain
This spot is our museum

Wish I could steal the key to those years
Take us back before we broke here

The love I had for you was deep
Some part of me still does

You were a rainbow in a life so grey
If only you felt the same as I

Maybe "us" was always meant to be doomed

For you, I was just someone to pass the time
For me, you were my everything

But this generation loves to play games
Hurting people's feelings for the fun of it
Multiple girls who are in their DM'S

That's where we are so different
I'll never be like that; I'll never be you

I am still sitting and wondering if you are with someone
Sending you a text to see if you care
But you don't because you have someone new

You say you don't, but I know you do
I know you more than you know

Your promises rot like rotten apples
Yet here I am still collecting in the garden

I remember the lies, replay the wrongs
My soul still reaches out for your hand
Why?

Maybe broken wounds miss their breaker

*Telling myself I don't care
Yet here I am still waiting*

*Telling myself I'm okay
Yet here I am still hurting*

*My mind is consumed by you daily
Does your mind catch a glimpse of me?*

*I say I've moved on
But deep down, that's a lie*

*I cared so much, but ...
You never cared about me*

The Recovery

My eyes are left dry from all the tears I have cried
They remember the pain caused
But forget how to weep

My heart aches in pain
But my body remains numb

Like frostbite without a pulse
Forced to hurt without a flinch

My mind again consumed by your ghost
There's a war in my head, going crazy

Wondering if I want the soldier to return
But your silence speaks loudly

Now I'm uncertain ...

5 days since I had a ping on my phone
You didn't miss my absence?
You're distracted by shiny new things

While my ghost lingers in the shadows
Hoping you catch a glimpse of me

How am I supposed to sleep
When you come and haunt my dreams

My mind is reminding me of the damage
But my heart is unable to forget

The millions of pieces you scattered
While my dreams try to collect the shards

Went for a drive today, and there you were
A live bomb was thrown across my path

My heart is pounding, waiting to be blown up
My body is trembling while it counts down

3
2
1
BOOM!

Here lies the broken heart of the pain you caused me

Unable to crawl out of my bed today
Yesterday was painful, and I'm numb

Part of me hoped to see your face
While the other part was trembling in pain

How do you erase someone whom you
Once shared memories
Now I have to mourn a person who's alive

*You told me I deserve better
But the saddest truth?*

*You could've been better
But you chose to be nothing*

*Was every "I love you"!
And every "I miss you"!*

Practice for someone else's story

Sitting here in our old spot, reminiscing about the days
Remembering the lies you said

Our old spot feels like a graveyard
Dead but with memories never forgotten

You were more to me than just a corpse
Now I'm left with everything we could've been

There's a letter in your mailbox
That envelope held my last hope

Those gifts I returned were not surrendered
They just held memories I couldn't forget

Choosing to heal myself
Instead of being haunted by a memorable treasure

We now board different planes
Each with our destinations

I'm left with all the baggage
While you just have your boarding pass

Now our separate journeys begin

Days drift slowly by, like the clock's not ticking
My heart is still full of love

Telling me I'll move on and forget you
As if it's changing your clothes daily

Like it's so easy to forget someone
You gave your whole heart to

*Dreamt of you last night
Even in my dreams, we are puppets
Dancing around each other's Games
Haunted by each other's suffering*

*I'm the host, waiting for the guest to arrive
But no guest comes..
While you have already invited your guest over*

Why were you at our old spot
I made this place my refuge

My sanctuary of safety and peace
That girl you brought here

Doesn't know this is our graveyard
The ground filled with my blood and tears

*My emotions gradually faded
While my love remained the same*

*You called me childish
Misread my caring for childishness*

*Took my jealousy as immature
And my words caused an uproar
That you wanted to silence*

Now you'll search for my noise in the silence

*Slowly drifting out of my mind
Like a plane leaving the airport*

*Late nights I spent wondering
How would it feel to forget you*

Weightless

Limitless

Free

*But look, here I am
Still moving along daily*

*Not broken, just healed
I don't miss you*

*I miss who I was before
I knew you existed*

One day, you'll see me walk past you
A stranger, changed and unrecognisable

The girl you once knew will be gone
I'll be happy, I won't even care to see you

You'll walk past me, and my emotions will be nothing

Sometimes you come to my mind
When you come to my mind, it's not the same anymore

No longer wondering what you are doing or who you text

You were on my mind for a second, then gone in a blink
Funny how you used to mean so much to me

I wake up feeling happy
I wake up, and the sadness is gone

I wake up with dry eyes
I wake up wanting to leave my bed

I wake up and know my life is wonderful
I wake up knowing life doesn't stop for anyone,
not even you

Hating you is something I could never do
Feeling grateful, the delusions are gone

You were the wrong person,
Now it is time for the right one
You sometimes still meet my mind

But now I know your actions weren't real
Wrong people lie, and that's who you are

*Slowly, you fade away from my brain
Then something reminds me of you*

Is this normal? Is this moving on?

*I slowly forget about you
But the world has other plans
Every day I'm reminded of you*

*Replaying old conversations in my head
Like they are song lyrics on a loop*

*I wonder to myself where I went wrong
Wondering if I could go back in time*

Did those old lyrics not mean something to you?

Some days, I sit and wait for a message
But the message never comes

I guess you moved on
You moved on because I never meant anything
I haven't moved on, I don't know if I will

You were my everything
You can't move on from someone whom you loved

*You made me feel like I was special
In the end, I never was I was just your object*

*You finally blocked me everywhere
You told me it was for the best*

*But the truth is, it was only best for you
Because in the end, you just used me*

I used to wish you the best, but now I don't
I hope someone hurts you like you hurt me

One day, you will realise how much I loved you
By that time, it'll be too late, I'll be moved on

I loved you, but you were another wrong person
Now I leave you and find who I deserve

www.ingramcontent.com/pod-product-compliance
Lightning Source LLC
Chambersburg PA
CBHW022018290426
44109CB00015B/1221